SEARCHING

The God you always wanted is really there.

Selected chapters from the bestseller,
"Searching for a God to Love" by Chris Blake

Pacific Press® Publishing Association
Nampa, Idaho
Oshawa, Ontario, Canada

Edited by Jerry D. Thomas
Designed by Robert Mason/Dennis Ferree

ISBN 0-8163-1847-6

01 02 03 04 05 • 5 4 3 2 1

To my first family of life and laughter,
Marise, Bruce, Alison, and Janine,
and to their loved ones

To the memory of my father,
James Harlan Blake

I don't know who God is. We're not up to that yet.

Elementary school student

There are many fine things which we cannot say if we have to shout.

Henry David Thoreau

I am astonished at the boldness with which people undertake to speak of God.

Blaise Pascal

Whether we recognize it or not, we begin as agnostics. If we do not acknowledge this, we will be too preoccupied with trivial gods to notice the real God standing before us.

Leslie Weatherhead

I cannot completely believe in a God that I can understand completely.

Lora Hagen

It's a great big universe and we're all really puny.

We're just tiny little specks about the size of Mickey Rooney.

Animaniacs

Who alone stretched out the heavens,
and trampled the waves of the sea;
who made the Bear and Orion,
the Pleiades, and the chambers of the south;
who does great things beyond understanding,
and marvelous things without number.
Lo, he passes by me, and I see him not;
he moves on, but I do not perceive him.

Job, *chapter 9*

The people who sat in darkness have seen a great light.

Jesus, quoting Isaiah

Excuse Me, You're Stepping on My God

For some reason, I felt like getting up. This isn't my typical early-Sunday feeling but that morning instead of bringing in the plump newspaper for a browse, I entered our dark family room, located the remote, and turned on the TV. During the first seven seconds, only sound emerged. A man was speaking—shouting, actually. His voice rose and fell as the screen's thousands of red, blue, and yellow pixels summoned the image of a televangelist.

Never before had I actually watched this show. The speaker paced the platform like a caged cat in a sleek blue suit, stalking and prancing, rumbling and wooing. With majestic emotion he told how "government and the media" collaborate in one evil conspiracy. He equated God's interests with America's interests, knew precisely God's plans and desires—the most intricate, God-smudged blueprints, the throbbing heart of life's great pulse—and claimed that everything happens "according to God's will." He carried God in his pocket.

At first I was merely amazed by the vastness of his narrowness. Slowly, though, my anger began to bubble. The sermon crawled with glittering generalities and yawning inaccuracies, quotations ripped from their context, opposing views clustered and characterized in the vilest light. Was his cause so good that he could behave so badly?

Following a crescendo summary, the preacher delivered an eyes-scrunched prayer that seemed directed toward the viewing audience. A moment after the "Amen," numbers galloped across the screen: "Call 1-800 . . ." Send money to "this address" to receive your "free gift." Visa, Discover, and MasterCard logos appeared. An announcer with a voice like dark syrup supplied details. The speaker returned to personally urge viewers to "give abundantly and be blessed abundantly." In conclusion, he looked out and with polished sincerity appealed that "the Lord would come right now into your heart."

It was at this point that a surprising conviction hit me. *Even if you're right about what you're saying, even if everything you say is true*, I thought, *I don't want it.*

I flicked off the set. The screen flashed and spat black.

▲ ▼ ▲

Colors.

As I sit in darkness in Griffith Park Planetarium in Los Angeles, that's what stuns me first. Kaleidoscopic magentas. Cool blues. Flaming oranges and stark whites. Jade and aqua, crimson and candlelight, dazzling colors wash in gauzy waves across the canvas of the universe.

Numbers.

More than 100 billion galaxies spiral in the void. The sky is thick with light, like dipping a toothbrush in white paint and thumbing the bristles over black velvet. Hold out a dime at arm's length: the coin covers 15 million stars in our Milky Way alone.

Some scientists estimate that a sun explodes with each tick of the clock. Infant stars, wrapped in linens of dust and gas, are born just as often. One tablespoonful of a neutron star would weigh about 5 trillion pounds on earth. "In the universe," writes Lao Tzu, "the difficult things are done as if they were easy."

Vastness.

Light travels 186,000 miles each second. At that speed a bullet rockets around Earth and grazes your ear seven times (ouch ouch ouch ouch ouch ouch ouch) in less than a second. The sun's light reaches us in 8.3 light-minutes. Neptune is about seven light-hours away. Andromeda, our closest spiral galaxy, is 2.2 million light-years away and stretches 100,000 light-years from edge to edge.

Gulp.

The lights come on, and I'm suddenly aware that my mouth hangs open. Leaving the planetarium, I pass the huge Foucault pendulum rocking from the lobby ceiling, monitoring our planet's predictable rotation. A car squeals out of the parking lot. Stepping outside, I stare straight up and drink in the whirling night. "The stars," observes Brennan Manning, "call us out of ourselves."

Then my thoughts turn to something truly wondrous. *Those intergalactic views are only half the picture.* Have you visited the Monsanto exhibit at the original Disneyland? There we're led to feel that we're shrinking to infinitesimal proportions—smaller, smaller, smaller. At one point an enormous human eye blinks at us through a microscope. Eventually we shrink into the center of an atom with its orbiting electrons and surging nucleus. In marvelous terror a voice cries out, "Dare I go on?" Some scientists claim we could go on, traveling deeper and deeper into the nucleus and its constituents. They also say that if you could harness and convert the energy, you could power your house for a day using the atoms in the period at the end of this sentence. The ink on an 8-by-11-inch sheet of paper would power 150,000 days, more than 400 years.

Who are we to think we can comprehend a trillionth part of this incredible power? How could anyone possibly know what animates galaxies and pulsates within each atom? In the polluted wake of some televangelists we may feel reticent to speak, worrying that the vastness of *our* narrowness will become apparent, but in every people group on earth the topic comes up. In French this power is called *Dieu.* In German it's *Gott.* In Spanish, *Dios.* In Hebrew it is *Elohim.* For Hindus it is *Brahman.* For Muslims, *Allah.* In another arena, the power is referred to as *Essence, Universal Mind, Life Force.*

In this book the power is called *God.* To many people—millions, probably—for myriad reasons "God" carries unpleasant associations. But a word is simply a symbol, not the object itself. By any other name a rose would smell as sweet, and by any other name God would still be, in Anselm's words, "That than which no greater can be conceived."

As a young child I attended Bethel Congregational Church, where every worship service Mr. Blakeslee, the organist, sat front and center behind a soft burgundy curtain. I could glimpse only the back of his bald, pale head. Somehow with my small eyes and ears watching and listening each week, I came to connect Mr. Blakeslee with God. God played unseen music with hidden hands and a mysterious face. Was He smiling or scowling? I had no clue. If I had chanced a guess based on the music, He would be minor-chord prone, majestic, gloomy, and loud.

For many of us who have carried similar images into adulthood, God remains inscrutable and distant. Is a grin playing on the lips, a tear moving, a glint of anger flashing? We try to discern the face of the player by the music, but all we know is the back of a bald head. We are also curious: What is this musician like away from the instrument and the score? Gentle? Petty? Vindictive? Fun-loving?

My friend Kim is thoughtful, fun, responsible, and skeptical. She's a believing unbeliever, one who believes in a God but who doesn't believe everything people say about God. At one time she "followed God," but too many things about that God didn't make sense, so she scrapped the whole idea. We talked last summer on the back of a houseboat one night when the Milky Way actually looked milky, and Kim questioned why any God would allow little children to suffer, and why God isn't more visible. After hearing about what she doesn't believe in, I asked her what she does believe in, at the core of her being.

"I guess I believe in Christian values," she said sheepishly, and we both laughed.

"That seems a bit strange," I suggested, "to believe in those values but not in the Being who established them."

"I just don't see another way around it right now," she admitted.

This book is about falling in love with God, and it's mostly for people like Kim. If you're an "unbeliever" who yearns for a God who is more than televangelists and traditional religion are communicating—indeed, more than anyone could communicate—this book is for you. Frederick Buechner points out, "Many an atheist is a believer without knowing it, just as many a believer is an atheist without knowing it. You can sincerely believe there is no God and act as if there is. You can sincerely believe there is a God and live as though there isn't."

If you're a "believer" who feels squeezed and drained by

a religious existence of deep weariness, unending frustration, and blasted hopes, to the point where even if your religion is "right" you don't know if you want it, this book is also for you.

Step one

Let's admit something from the start: we cannot know God.

Agnostics contend we cannot know God. Often they say this because of God's transcendent nature, as caterpillars cannot know humans. Caterpillars can *experience* humans. They can crawl fuzzily up our fingers and forearms and swivel their heads quizzically, but they cannot *know* us because we transcend them.

But let's admit we don't *know* even the people we live with. How deeply does a husband know his wife? How much do we know our parents, our children, our friends? The more we know, the more we suspect that we know very little. Like the six blind men of Indostan "reading" a Braille elephant, we know in part at best. The wonder is that even when we cannot know fully, we can love wholeheartedly. That which we do know—the kernel of a person that makes a person—we love. We believe Forrest Gump when he proclaims, "I'm not a smart man, but I know what love is." We can and we do love the unfathomable.

Our search for understanding God can produce only more confusion. When *Life* magazine asked forty-nine obscure and famous people the ultimate question "Why are we here?" Garrison Keillor replied, "To know and to serve God, of course, is why we're here, a clear truth that, like the nose on your face, is near at hand and easily discernible but can make you dizzy if you try to focus on it hard." To their credit, many agnostics don't wish to strap God to any human framework. They maintain that any limitation we place on God is illusory; any claim to "know God" seems arrogant and naive. We are too feeble, too finite.

A short story describes beings in a distant galaxy whose home planet is warmed by multiple suns. Night never falls. While life in this sphere is fine enough, a terrible mystery consumes the thoughts of all inhabitants. Every six hundred years the suns align in one monstrous eclipse, plunging the planet for a few hours into total darkness, and each time this happens, according to historical records, nearly all the inhabitants are wiped out. What is it about the darkness that proves fatal?

At last the moment of the eclipse arrives, and the inhabitants witness a startling sight. They see, for the first time, stars. Thousands upon thousands of shimmering stars. The vision sends them over the edge to insanity or to suicide. Why? Because suddenly they comprehend their true insignificance in the universe. They are a microscopic speck in a chartless ocean, a whimper in a hurricane, an M&M in the Milky Way.

The agnostic view does take into account our puny proportions and humble perspective when compared to God. However, agnosticism can actually end up limiting God. For it is true: we cannot know God ... *unless God chooses to be known.* In prematurely ending that sentence, the agnostic view steps on God by restricting this option. Can our knowledge of God be objectively measured? Not really. But neither can we objectively measure truth, hope, or compassion.

Imagine a young man interviewing for a high-paying job with a major corporation. He slides through two interviews, shuffles past the formidable executive secretary, and finds himself face-to-face with the founder, owner, and CEO of the corporation. After exchanging pleasantries, the young man speaks his mind.

"I know you're in control here," he offers generously, "so I want you to know something. You can do *anything* you like!"

"Oh . . . um . . . thanks," the owner manages to say.

"Unless," the young man continues, "you want to communicate personally with me or with any of your employees. That, of course, is impossible."

"Excuse me?"

"Well, you can't do *that.* You're too far above us. We can't appreciate you for all that you truly are."

At this point the owner assures the young man that he won't have to concern himself further with the prospect, and she escorts him to the door.

It's possible to hold mistaken assumptions about the "owner," isn't it? If an Owner God decides to communicate with us, who are we to deny that privilege? We can't enable caterpillars to know or love us, but (this is an important point) we aren't God. We created neither caterpillar nor cosmos. Moreover, humans can comprehend infinitely more than caterpillars. As we explore later, God finds ingenious ways to interact with us.

Even with the best intentions, by denying God's ability or desire to communicate with us, we "step on" God.

Step two

I enjoy running. That's when I do my best thinking, away from the madding crowd. At least I think I do. When my family lived one mile from Pismo Beach, California, I would run three mornings a week. Stepping out my front door, I'd pad down the hills of Brighton Avenue, circle a fence that confined a snarling dog, dodge through some firs, cut over the railroad tracks, zip across Highway 1, and be on the beach. Easy.

Once there, I felt as if I could run for hours. The wide white sand lay flat and firm, giving gently to my strides. The early morning fog would be lifting against the hills, the seagulls gliding and calling, the moist air suffused with salt and seaweed. Ahead of me sandpipers raced the spreading foam, their skinny legs a blur. Often I passed people on the beach—lovers walking hand in hand, another runner, a solitary soul thinking deeply, arms crossed, head down, and no matter who it was, I always called out, "Morning!" Nearly always I received a somewhat surprised smile and a greeting in return.

One morning a man didn't return my greeting. He stood alone, hidden in a heavy coat and gloves, but different from most beach walkers. He was inhaling a cigarette and listening intently to his headphones, swinging a metal detector across the sand like the sightless wield a white cane. I called out "Morning!" and waved. He never noticed.

I understood his not wanting to hear or see the gasping, dripping man plodding by, but in hearing only his headphones he was missing the rhythmic roar of the surf and the squawking gulls. Looking only at his feet, he lost the splendor of the sandpipers and the lifting fog. With his coat and mind tightly buttoned, he could not appreciate invigorating sensations all around him. He could never find with Shakespeare "tongues in trees, books in running brooks, sermons in stones and good in everything."

Too often we are like that man, swinging into God's revelations and not perceiving them. As Job confesses, "He passes by me, and I see him not." If we listen merely for life's metallic beeping, how can God get through? Our frantic society's beeps—the financial pressures of the long, green madness and 1:15 appointments and advertising blitzes and bizarre relationship problems and every last honking hurry—can overwhelm us.[1] We lose the ability to make sense. We lose the ability to perceive.

We step on God when we become so busy and bothered that we do not discern that God is here.

Step three

It's another misty morning, another run. Approaching me on the far side of the street walks a raven-haired wisp of a girl, about eleven years old, carrying a pink lunch bag and three books.

"Morning!" I call to her, and I smile.

Her response isn't one I'm used to. Lowering her eyes, her body tenses and she quickens her pace. She's clearly afraid.

Of course, she's right. Someone has taught her well: Don't talk to strangers. But I'm angry as I move beyond her. No, not at her. I'm angry with the people who took away an eleven-year-old girl's freedom to smile without fear and sing out, "Good morning!" I'm incensed with those who by their hideous actions spawned an epidemic of distrust.

Let's switch scenes. I'm talking with someone I know—he's a friend. During the course of our easy conversation I mention the word *God*. Instantly his face stiffens, his eyes glaze over. It's obvious he wants no part of this discussion. His expression clearly tells me, *Let's forget about that, OK?*

And at once our freedom has been pinched. Our liberty to go beyond the banalities of bad weather, ball scores, and inevitable air disasters has been stepped on. We can't explore the meaning of life with candor and good humor in a nonthreaten-

---

1. Poet e. e. cummings refers to "this busy monstermanunkind."

ing atmosphere. We just can't. The possibility is gone. Vanished.

That scene is replayed on this planet a thousand times a day. I'm angry with those who bred this discomfort, this reluctance bordering on abhorrence. Who caused these responses?

Mostly, religious people caused them.

Let me be clear in defining what I mean here by "religious people." I mean slippery, pushy evangelists attempting to cram others into their view of salvation. Deliver us from them.

I mean careful churchgoers who care more about raising money than about raising literacy rates. Those who "disdain the world" but crave its publicity. Those behind vanilla smiles who see no relevance in healing a poisoned environment, or in developing better housing for the poor, or in upholding the rights and dignity of minorities.

I mean those who deny the true power of God and instead use church as a social coffee club, where the elite meet to greet. I mean those who distort and manhandle the Bible to the point where onlookers give up trying to make any sense of it.

I mean religious entertainers, including many neighborhood pulpit-pounders, with their embarrassing, superficial antics. I mean those whose worship is all froth, and those whose worship is as flat as road kill at rush hour. I mean hate- and pride-filled fanatics, from Belfast to Bosnia to the West Bank, who pulverize one another in the name of God.

I mean those who want to look good, and who look the other way if someone else doesn't. I mean those who claim that the God of colors and numbers and vastness in the universe gets wrathful if a teenage girl wears too much makeup. I could go on. You know what I mean.

Of course, religionists don't own a corner on bad behavior.

(If you have trouble believing this, just pick up today's newspaper.) Unfortunately, however, religionists' actions are often connected to God. All of us at some time are embarrassed by our connections, whether our workplace, our political party, our country, our race, our favorite athletes or musicians, our family. In our more lucid moments, we don't simply write these connections off. We understand that reality and the ideal don't often mesh. But with so many things in the world poised to go wrong, we're looking for connections that bring lasting peace of mind.

How I wish I could adequately communicate this: *God's seekers are turned off to "religion" more than anybody.* "Religion" robs me of being able to talk with friends and relatives about my greatest love, my God. That's why, to a Christian God-seeker, it makes no sense to hear that someone isn't interested in God because she's "turned off by religion."

According to a recent Gallup poll, people today are increasingly more interested in spiritual things. I found this to be true when walking through Chicago's O'Hare Airport with the book *God: A Biography* tucked under my arm. While I stood in lines, travelers craned their necks to read the dust jacket, commenting on the fascinating nature of the concept. People today are interested in God. They are wary and weary of religionists. We step on God when we reduce God to a pre-packaged agenda, to a set of religious precepts easily held and manipulated.

It is possible to step on the limitless God of the universe to the place where not only can God not be found, but nobody's even looking.

TWO

Stalking the Wild Truth

The needles, the tubes, the beeping chrome monitors, all filled her with horror. Sylvia harbored a paralyzing dread of life-support systems. While visiting a friend who was in a hospital, however, she determined to bravely steel herself. As she walked through the disinfected halls she tried not to peek at the machines in the rooms.

It was no use. She needed to get out. Trembling, she reached the nearest elevator and stabbed the down button. When the elevator door opened, a hospital attendant stood beside a gleaming chrome machine covered with tubes and dials. Sylvia hesitated, swallowed, and stepped inside. The door closed. She gazed straight ahead, her face a mask of apprehension. At last she blurted, "I sure would hate to be hooked up to one of those!"

The attendant looked down at the machine and up at Sylvia. "So would I," he said evenly. "It's a rug cleaner."

Life is full of illusions. We run from we-know-not-what to the arms of the comfortable unknown. Even the language we use to clarify life can be tricky. Customers enter a hair salon to receive a permanent, and six months later they return for another. Doctors attend medical school so they can finally practice, but I really don't want a doctor to *practice* on me. People declare, "It goes without saying that . . ." and then they say it. Or they write, "not to mention . . ." and then mention it. Moreover, speakers talk about what they'd like to do as if it's being done. They announce, "We'd like to welcome you here tonight" or "I'd like to thank everyone who made this possible," and I think, *Well, then, go ahead and do it.* It seems that in the entire history of the Academy Awards no one has ever actually thanked anyone for anything, though they'd like to.

Perhaps no word in the English language is freighted with more hidden meanings than the word *love.* So when we talk of loving God, do we mean the love of "I love mashed potatoes," "love is a many-splendored thing," or "love your enemies?" Maybe this love is a quick infatuation heard best in the classic song lyric, "Hello, I love you, won't you tell me your name?" Or could it be tugging curiosity, as with the hundreds who flocked to see the face of Jesus on a burned tortilla, and the thousands who viewed the image of the Virgin Mary on the concrete floor of a shower stall in a bathroom of Progreso Auto Supply in Progreso, Texas?[1]

Our ideas of love and God depend on our perceptions. Common wisdom holds that our minds are like parachutes, functioning only when open, but it's also possible to be so open-minded that our brains fall out. The story is told of Samuel Taylor Coleridge receiving a visitor who advised, "Don't teach your children what to believe. Let them grow up free to choose for themselves." Coleridge took him out to the "garden," a weedy, thistle-strewn patch of earth. The visitor was stunned. "You call this a

---

1. I've often wondered how people "recognize" these likenesses. Are original photographs somewhere in existence?

garden?" he fumed. "There's nothing here but weeds!"

"That's true," Coleridge replied, "I thought, however, that I would leave the flowers free to choose for themselves."

This garden we call modern society can appear overgrown. Wisdom of generations lies tangled and buried. The weeds inherit the earth. We grow up devotees of a vapid anythink. G. K. Chesterton concludes, "When a man ceases to believe in God, he does not believe in nothing, he believes in anything."

One night I was talking with a close friend, and we got around to our beliefs on spiritual matters. He mentioned a belief he endorsed, and I wondered aloud how it measured up to reality, how it made sense.

"It doesn't have to make sense," he said.

My mind somersaulted. *If it doesn't have to make sense, then what ultimately matters?* Why not believe that flossing teeth brings salvation? Why not worship *TV Guide* or a jar of mayonnaise? We may as well follow Adolf Hitler or David Koresh, or be one of Marshall Applewhite's conscientious corpses wearing new Nikes. Certainly we don't comprehend all of our senses, and much of our "sensible" thinking is nonsense, yet on what basis do we make any decisions at all? Do we amputate our brains when we enter spiritual discussions?

Many of our ideas arrive courtesy of pop culture; we got our politics from Hollywood, and we're getting our religion from Hollywood, our views on life and afterlife. I've lost count of how many films, from *Steel Magnolias* to *Titanic,* depict "religious" characters as odd in some way, but when actress Shirley MacLaine proclaims, "*You* are God. *You* know you are divine," her opinion is accepted by millions as natural and credible.

Too often we inherit our thoughts from seeing only the obvious; our sponge souls soak in what makes direct contact. In seeing superficially we miss how life is not as much either/or as it is both/and—fair and unfair, parched and moist, complex and simple. Each semester at the start of Freshman Composition, my college students encounter a twenty-five-second experiment in seeing, where they look at the following diagram and simply count the number of squares. Try it for yourself.

Some students shoot me a peek after three seconds that says, "Yeah, now what?" Then, glancing around, they notice others inspecting the figure, and look again. Many are still counting when the twenty-five seconds elapse. While I scribble numbers on the board the class calls out how many squares they saw.

"Twenty-one!"

"Nineteen!"

"Twenty-five!"

"Thirty!"

"Thirty-two!"

By this time *all* the students are intently studying the square. What seemed so obvious at first is suddenly . . . different. I trace the thirty squares (yes, thirty). "Those of you who found more than thirty are into another dimension," I add, and we laugh. The point of the exercise will be brought to their attention many times during the course: *Be more than a sixteen-square person.* We discuss how those who found sixteen, twenty-one, and twenty-five squares were *right* as far as they went, and how there's more to life than being *right*. As John Fischer told me, "An artist is one who stays a little longer." When we look at a tree, for instance, and see it merely as a tree, we miss a sanctuary; a living sculpture; a food source for woodpeckers, insects, and giraffes; a shade producer; a musical instrument in a breeze; a rooted tower; a means of transportation; a paper factory; a micro-organic nursery of wriggling newborns; a source of poetry; a playmate; and dozens more. Looking beyond the obvious requires purposeful effort, particularly when the figure we're studying is "God."

Some people can look at the diagram for a month and see only sixteen squares. They stop looking, believing that once they are *right* they no longer need to seek, and thereafter muddle through life in the light of a ten-watt bulb.[2] In addition, those who located thirty are in greatest peril, because they now perceive that they are completely in the right. Religionists see themselves often as thirty-square people, along with scientists and stockbrokers, professors and postal workers, computer technicians and cabbies, and thus we shut ourselves off from seeing—in seeing, we become blinded.

Zealots and commentators of God leave us wondering if we can see even sixteen squares. In place of a pale bald head, God is an oblong gray blur. The image morphs and fades. Seeking a God to control, we create God in our own image, as seen in the ending of Robert Ku's poem "God in the Box":

---

2. None is so blind as one who will not see.

"pity./ I have given God/ my Social Security number./ I call God/ with a toll-free number./ I make Him into a fast-food/ drive-in./ I wait for Him to ask,/ may I help you, please?/ so I can answer,/ two Cokes and a good life/ to go."

In the midst of running from rug cleaners and chasing after charred tortillas, could we pause from our illusions to consider another view of reality?

Reality is not always multiple choice

I stared into the blue-white of retreating Mendenhall Glacier outside Juneau, Alaska. My brother Bruce was describing how the seven-story ice calves into the bay, creating enormous ripples, exposing blue flesh like an open wound. It doesn't happen often. In fact, he said, though he visits the glacier fairly frequently, he has never witnessed a calving. Then he related an unsettling tale.

A daring young man and woman a few years back decided to picnic near the edge of the glacier. They stumbled across the ice, threw down a blanket and a basket, and began enjoying their *alfresco* summer meal together, virtually dangling their feet over the cliff of ice. After a few delightful minutes, a terrific *crack* rent the air. While onlookers watched in horror, tons of ice under the couple collapsed into the frigid tidal lake. Their bodies were never recovered.

I stared once more at the massive glacier, then peered at Bruce. "Really?" I sputtered. "No way! That sounds like an urban legend."

"I understand that it happened," said Bruce somberly, "right there."

Of the many lessons that could be gleaned from this story, one stands pre-eminent. What the couple believed about the glacier didn't matter. In the end, all that mattered was the objective reality of the glacier. All their beliefs merged with reality as they dropped to the booming water.

This lesson runs counter to Gustave Flaubert's new-age creed, "The only reality is perception." Flaubert's statement acknowledges the complexity of life and our bewilderment with it, along with the power of perception. When I teach communication courses we make use of this power by examining and comparing our perceptions, and surely our perceptions create a vision of reality for us. Without delving to bottomless philosophical depths, the danger lies in extrapolating the vision until we believe that no objective reality therefore exists.[3] This illusion is particularly prevalent when people speak of God as simply a subjective extension of our egos, projecting our own desires. "If that's God to you, fine," our society affirms. "Whatever works, honey."

What difference does it make what we think of God? Quite literally, all the difference in the world. Our view of reality is anchored in our view of God. For some the sour breath of life—the morning breath of God—permeates a lifetime. Whatever we worship does become God to us. But as with glaciers, an inexorable reality prevails.

Once a five-year-old girl brought a baby rabbit to her kindergarten class for show-and-tell. She had already dragged the box down two aisles when suddenly a fellow classmate wondered aloud, "What is this rabbit, a boy or a girl?"

The show-er couldn't tell. She looked to the teacher for help, but the teacher was at a loss for words. Relief came in the form of a small hand raised in the back. "I

---

3. One of the problems the relativist faces is his belief that only his theory is absolute.

know, teacher!" offered the student. "Let's vote on it!"

Quiddity is a philosophical term meaning the essential nature of an object—what something actually *is.* Quiddity bangs against the worldview of let's-vote-on-it reality. Naturally, we don't whistle Flaubert's tune whenever we approach a traffic stoplight or ask for a bank withdrawal, because perception is not enough, then. "I thought it should have been green" or "Maybe I missed a few digits" doesn't cut it. In real life, a smorgasbord of choose-your-own realities is unacceptable whenever we deeply care about the results. We know better. Maylan Schurch notes how the universe (including God) works logically and predictably once we understand valid premises.[4]

> Twelve years ago NASA aimed *Voyager 2* on a billion-mile space flight, knowing that Neptune would swing around to the target spot just when *Voyager* got there. And sure enough, Neptune swung out, blue and beautiful, ready to pose for the cameras.
>
> And here on earth, things are logical too. Cause leads to effect billions of times a day. Sperms and eggs unite, cells grow, babies develop. Injury causes pain. Food digests. People grow and fall in love. Cause leads to effect again and again.

In Bangkok, Thailand, you can buy Peanuts apparel with a dog named "Snooby," polo shirts carrying the label "Ralph Laurence," and authentic Western wear from "Lavish Strauss." However, you would never know they aren't the genuine ar-

---

4. The strange world of quantum reality and the chaos theory notwithstanding.

ticle if you didn't know the genuine article. A fake can be hard to detect. Police experts in recognizing counterfeit money explain that the best way they ascertain a fake is to keep studying the original, to become so adept in the true currency that they know it by heart.

Studying a real God leads to authenticity. Any time we hear of those "called by God" to murder for peace, deceive for truth, or demean for love, we recognize a counterfeit. It's also well to remember that we would have no counterfeits without the genuine. Following the genuine God brings us a well-rounded life of physical, mental, and emotional balance. Keeping our balance, as G. K. Chesterton attests, is a challenging endeavor:

> It is always simple to fall; there are an infinity of angles at which one falls, only one at which one stands. To have fallen into any one of the [current] fads . . . would indeed have been obvious and tame. But to have avoided them all has been one whirling adventure; and in my vision the heavenly chariot flies thundering through the ages, the dull heresies sprawling and prostrate, the wild truth reeling and erect.

Stalking the wild truth

An obviously inebriated man was crawling under a street lamp at three A.M. Gliding by in his car, a police officer called out, "Hey, what are you doing there? Do you need some help?"

"I'm l-looking for my wallet," explained the man. "I l-lost it . . . on the corner of Third and Elm."

"Third and Elm?" exclaimed the officer. "This is Ninth and Spruce!"

"I know," the man replied. "But the l-light is better here."

We don't have to be drunk to pursue the truth about God where the "light is better." Human beings by nature gravitate toward an easy place, even if it's nowhere near the truth. In "The Wayfarer," Stephen Crane accurately describes our inclination:

The wayfarer,
Perceiving the pathway to truth,
Was struck with astonishment.
It was thickly grown with weeds.
"Ha," he said,
"I see that none has passed here
In a long time."
Later he saw that each weed
Was a singular knife.
"Well," he mumbled at last,
"Doubtless there are other roads."

Do we really want to get in touch with an objective reality? Do we aim toward the scintillating light of truth, joy, and freedom, or have we grown so dependent on our lies, our pains, and our prisons that any light is blinding and we seek the comfort of familiar cold shadows?

I once had a student who was struggling with incredible pain; she had been sexually abused as a child, yet she still had to face the relative who had abused her. Though her life was unraveling and she recognized the need for help, she shunned counseling. Rather, she made appointments with a counselor and never kept them. Watching her slide lower and lower, I felt powerless because she would not honestly confront her problem and help herself.

One day as she was leaving class, I called her to the front and handed her a note with the simple message, "John 5:6." The scene portrayed in this verse involves Jesus and a man who had been ill thirty-eight years. "When Jesus saw him and knew that he had been lying there a long time, he said to him, 'Do you want to be healed?' "

The next class, I sensed that she was different. After class she approached my desk and said with a glowing peace, "You'll never know how much that note meant to me."

The key for all of us is courageous honesty, an attribute easier eulogized than lived out. Am I brave enough to follow truth where it leads? We must be committed to honesty before we can make any changes in our opinion of God. When the groundbreaking book *The Day America Told the Truth* was written based on surveys across the United States, the published results stunned readers everywhere. Survey respondents had been advised, "We don't want surface answers to these questions. We don't want white lies. Please. No white lies. . . . We are looking for total honesty." This advice rose to sublime irony in the section on honesty, where the authors discovered that "Americans . . . lie more than we had ever thought possible before the study. . . . Lying has become an integral part of the American culture, a trait of the American character. We lie and don't even think about it. We lie for no reason. The writer Vance Bourjaily once said, 'Like most men, I tell a hundred lies a day.' That's about right. And the people we lie to most are those closest to us." We don't even need to open our mouths to lie; an arched eyebrow, a pause, a slight nod can communicate volumes of misleading information. "The cruelest lies," Robert Louis Stevenson reflects, "are often told in silence."

How can we make contact with reality when we swim in an ocean of lies? Construction workers, accountants, politicians, and parents shamelessly distort the truth. Television comedies follow a stock formula: sticky predicament . . . lie . . . big laugh. Nearly every episode of *I Love Lucy,* the mother of all TV sitcoms, bounces from deception to deception, and though Fred, Ethel, Ricky and Lucy learn a lesson in the end, the moral has been drained. Audiences don't regard falsehood as truly destructive when they're holding their sides with laughter.

The truth is often painful to look in the face. I witnessed this in my father's U. S. history classroom when I visited one day and noticed a sophomore tapping her pencil on sheet after sheet of paper for the entire period. After class I asked Dad what she was doing. He told me that he had been attempting to impress upon students the immensity of the number 1,000,000,000, because people tend to talk about billions of dollars in a fairly offhanded way. He promised that anyone who made a billion marks during the semester would receive an automatic 'A.' He had the class make marks as fast as they could for one minute, then calculate how long it would take them, working for twelve hours each day, seven days a week, to reach one billion. (A constant rate of three marks per second, or 129,600 marks per day, would require 7,716 days— about twenty-one years.)

"So, why is she still doing it?" I asked.

Dad shook his head sadly. "Because, she told me, she wants an 'A' in this class. And she said she was willing to work more than twelve hours a day on it." He held up a fistful of papers covered with marks. "She's already done more than ten million. I've showed her the math and proved that she can never make it, but she keeps tapping her days away."

Confronted with the truth, many people react fearfully and illogically. One definition of a fanatic is someone who, once the error of his ways has been clearly demonstrated, redoubles his efforts in the same direction. The bold success of Alcoholics Anonymous and spinoff twelve-step recovery groups is predicated on honesty.[5] What changes the groups? Total honesty. The truth is elevating, the truth is humbling. The truth is stratospheric, the truth is earthbound. Anything less than truth results in wrecked lives.

How does being committed to truth lead to loving God? If our sincere quest is not toward total honesty and truth, we will wander in forests of deceptions, looking where the light is "better" and endlessly tapping on meaningless papers. What is acceptable we accept; we almost never do the unthinkable. If worshiping figments and loving fakes is just fine, if lying appears to be an acceptable way of life, our spiritual compass will be continually spinning. In *Jeremiah* God laments, "They bend their tongue like a bow; falsehood and not truth has grown strong in the land; for they proceed from evil to evil, and they do not know me, says the Lord. . . . Heaping oppression upon oppression, and deceit upon deceit, they refuse to know me . . . You will seek me and find me when you seek me with all your heart, I will be found by you."[6]

Among the disturbing findings in *The Day America Told the Truth* is that nearly half the population honestly feel nobody knows them. Furthermore, one in four among us answered "nobody" to the question, "Who's for real?" If we aren't

5. The fifth step of the AA program reads, "Acknowledged to God, another human being and myself the exact nature of my wrongs."
6. Chapters 9 and 29.

for real, if we aren't seeking the real, how can God be there for us? In addition to fracturing human trust, here is the most devastating aspect of posing and dissembling: God cannot *find* us to heal us, to save us.[7] When God appears, we aren't home. Some other person, some wavy, porous public image, inhabits our bony frame.

Making contact can be unnerving. C. S. Lewis explains, "There comes a moment when the children who have been playing at burglars will hush suddenly: was that a *real* footstep in the hall? There comes a moment when people who have been dabbling in religion . . . suddenly draw back. Suppose we really found Him? We never meant it to come to *that!*" A friend told me he once knelt and prayed fervently for God's blessing and filling. Warm, dazzling light instantly enveloped him. Terrified, he opened his eyes and saw through the window before him that swift, dark clouds had exposed the naked sun. Reflecting on his fear when his request seemed actually granted, he confessed, "I'm not as cavalier about praying as I once was."

As is the case with real love, the wild truth leaves us confused, breathless with wide-eyed wonder, and liberated. The truth is as untamed as Einstein's hair, emphatic as a thunderhead, prickly as a sea urchin with an attitude. It is also a warm towel after a shower, clover to the brown-eyed cow, the last piece in a jigsaw puzzle, a child's kiss. The closer we get to truth, the closer we get to paradox. We learn that we must give to gain, serve to lead, be humble to be great. At the very least, truth startles us from our complacency. In his legendary commencement address to Duke University, Ted Koppel

7. In the Garden of Eden, Adam and Eve "hid themselves from the presence of the Lord God," and an all-seeing God asked, "Where are you?"

declared that "in its purest form, truth is not a polite tap on the shoulder. It is a howling reproach. What Moses brought down from Mount Sinai were not the Ten Suggestions."

Need I need need?

How do we know God exists? Can we know that we're not alone here?

Human beings are remarkably open to different paths of knowing. We may use empirical methods, memory, comparison, and intuition, but nothing surpasses one avenue of knowledge we use to know a bicycle or a houseplant. How do you know what you're sitting on right now will support you? How does a friend know that a job will be good for her? The best way to be certain is to test it. When *New York* magazine sent John R. Coleman into the streets of the city for ten days to pose as a homeless man, he opened his report:

> Somehow, twelve degrees at 6 am was colder than I had counted on. I think of myself as relatively immune to cold, but standing on a deserted sidewalk outside Penn Station with the thought of ten days ahead of me as a homeless man, the immunity vanished. When I pulled my collar closer and my watch cap lower, it wasn't to look the part of a street person; it was to keep the wind out.

We may resort to all types of theories *about* God, but the best way to be certain about God is to experience God, as billions have done in the midst of splintering grief and soaring ecstasy. This comes even to people who don't believe in God. C. S. Lewis confesses that while he was an atheist he not only maintained that God did not exist, but he was also very angry with God for not existing, and was equally angry with God for creating this world.

How important is testing our experience? Parents and teachers think that if we can persuade others to *believe* the right things, they will *act* the right way. But studies don't support this. Bill McNabb writes, "In 1964 psychologist Leon Festinger concluded that research had in fact not supported the assumption that people's attitudes or beliefs will change their behavior. Festinger and others advanced the radical notion that the attitude-behavior relationship actually works the other way around—that is, people are more likely to behave their way into thinking than think their way into behaving." We *believe what we do* more than we do what we believe. Cognitive dissonance dictates that we cannot continue to do something and persist in believing it's wrong; rather, we rationalize whatever we're doing.

McNabb points out, "One week of building houses for poor families is worth five years of Bible studies on the importance of Christian service. We have taken with us scores of teenagers who did not believe in Jesus' admonition to serve, but came to believe it by doing it." Standing outside and looking hard at God will not convince us; we come to know the path by stepping into the jungle. Action creates belief. Jesus insists, "Where your treasure is, there will your heart be also."

Knowing also goes beyond our senses. I once overheard a woman remark, "I've never seen God, and I can't believe in anything I can't see, hear, taste, smell, or touch." Sipping her Diet Pepsi, she concluded with a shrug, "So, I don't believe in God." At which point I wondered, *Have you ever seen a calorie? Or touched a calorie? How does a calorie taste?* As with all of us, she has yet to *experience* a calorie, yet calories fill conversations and dominate ad space, disappearing in everything from bathing suits to lite beer.

Though we can't see, hear, smell, taste, or touch calories, we believe in them. If calories function as a measurement of energy, what serves as a measurement for God? Typically we look toward tangible experiences as evidence of God's involvement (which can be as easy as seeing grass grow), but a major obstacle to measuring God arises if we judge on the basis of "good" events only. An American football player kneels in the end zone after a touchdown to thank God, yet could God be just as much in his fumble or dropped pass? Imagine a player kneeling after being thrown for a five-yard loss to pray, "Thank You, God, for keeping me humble. With all the hype, I need all the help I can get." We would know he was "shaken up."

James F. Sennett muses, " 'If it works, that must be God blessing it.' So stated, no intelligent Christian would endorse this motto." The problem with if-it-works religion is that people hold such bizarre ideas of what and why something "works." We chalk up our good fortune to lucky clothes and numbers, planets aligning, and miracle food supplements, yet when we do acquire our desire and it turns out to be a terrible mistake, we distrust God all the more. When the economy crashes, the atmosphere buckles under stress, and violent gangs terrorize suburbia, blame God. Our reasoning is akin to my enduring a sneezing fit for thirty minutes and then, instead of finding out what it is I'm allergic to, blaming the attack on my breathing. Obviously this breathing in—this inspiration—doesn't work for me.

The critical issue is need. Am I so self-absorbed that I stop looking at sixteen squares, believing that all I see is all that exists? Are my needs what the yelping advertisers insist? Here is a subtle foe. It's harder to feel our true need of God when a home entertainment center sits panting in the den. Houses, cars, clothes, computers, and snacks cushion and divert us from recognizing real needs until a romantic breakup or traffic accident wreathes us in smoke, reminding us of life's fundamentals.

Modern western society is afflicted by the curse of comfort, but our condition is nothing new. In the ancient book *Deuteuronomy*, Moses warns his people to beware, "lest, when you have eaten and are full, and have built goodly houses and live in them, and when your herds and flocks multiply, and your silver and gold are multiplied, then your heart be lifted up, and you forget the Lord your God."[8] Fifteen hundred years later a being "like a son of man" says to the church of Laodicea, representing our age, "You say, I am rich, I have prospered, and I need nothing, not knowing that you are wretched, pitiable, poor, blind, and naked."[9]

We should make a distinction between the conceit of believing we don't need God and the conceit of believing God favors us. Christians can fit into the latter category, but going to church is not a surefire sign of this conceit. A lunch partner once said to me, "What bothers me is that Christians think they have an inside path to God. That's so arrogant!"

I asked, "What do you think about God?"

He pointed to his chest. "God is right here, inside me."

"H'mm," I said. "Christians are arrogant because they feel their need enough to look to an outside God to heal them, but you *are* God. And they're the arrogant ones." He kept stirring his coffee.

---

8. Chapter 8.
9. In *Revelation,* chapter 3.

Going to church is no more spiritually arrogant than going for a walk is physically arrogant. The church is not a *Showtime!* for the saints but a hospital for the sick. It's a community designed to study and pursue deep quests of where we came from, who we are, where we're going. It's also a sanctuary for the bypassed, battered, baffled, and burned out. Because we're wretched and pitiable, doesn't mean we should stop visiting the hospital; in fact, in visiting the Doctor we more fully sense our needs. As He presses on our soul and inquires, "Does it hurt here?" we groan, and He says, "Take this medicine. You need to apply this salve."

We're all hurting. Every being on earth is fighting some type of uphill battle. Mike Yaconelli, a popular speaker on the Christian circuit, tells of agreeing to a friend's request that Yaconelli speak to the Northern California Toastmasters. Arriving at the event ten minutes before he was to speak, Yaconelli asked his friend to tell him a little more about the audience. His friend replied, "These people are the postmasters from every city in Northern California."

"*Post*masters?" I said rather sheepishly. "I thought you said *Toast*masters. *TOAST*masters!"

"No," he said, "why would I say that? I'm a postmaster."

I had ten minutes to formulate the keynote address for the Northern California Postmasters. I wasn't allowed to talk about God or Jesus, of course, but I certainly didn't have much to say about the new bulk mail regulations. I did the only thing I could do, I decided to speak about issues we all struggle with—loneliness, insignificance, and meaninglessness. In other words, I decided to talk about our common longings.

I was shocked.

There were tears in many of their eyes during the talk, and I received a standing ovation when it was over . . . and I discovered something that day: People are longing for God. I had inadvertently touched base with their longings. They knew the loneliness I was talking about. They were experiencing the meaninglessness and insignificance of much of their lives, and they could not hold back the tears.

We are lonely for God. Our longing goes beyond knowing *about* God: we want to *know* God, to find a companionable friend beyond the noise.[10] Above all, our need for a God to love draws us. "When the conversation moves to the subject of knowing God," Tim Stafford observes, "listeners grow suddenly quiet and attentive. For a long time I thought this was a disapproving silence. I now know it is the silence that falls on a room of hungry people when someone talks of food."

The bouts about doubt

Doubts have driven millions from God and steered millions toward God. Most of us hold healthy reservations on what we hear about God; doubtless we can become fanatical, woodenheaded, and self-serving.

Many commentators have expressed their views on doubt, particularly toward what appear to be God's startling concessions. Ellen White maintains, "God has never removed the possibility of doubt. Our faith must rest upon evidence, not

10. Milton writes, "Loneliness is the first thing which God's eye nam'd not good."

demonstration. Those who wish to doubt will have opportunity; while those who really desire to know the truth will find plenty of evidence on which to rest their faith." Frederick Buechner points out the dilemma we pose for God in demanding both certainty and personal freedom: "Without somehow destroying me in the process, how could God reveal Himself in a way that would leave no room for doubt? If there were no room for doubt, there would be no room for me." God would rather deal with rebels than robots.

Of course, in the matter of faith there is no convincing some people. "Doubt becomes a way of life just as faith does," Calvin Miller writes. "Hardcore skeptics have often fallen in love with arguing as a lifestyle. They don't want to be convinced by the practical nature of the Christian faith. Argumentation is their greatest joy. Becoming a Christian would eliminate the argument and ruin their fun." And so the skeptic's challenge is set forth: "Explain God!" While to a large degree God is eminently logical and sensible, He cannot be reduced to a formula or encompassed by an explanation.[11] It is impossible for finite minds to fully comprehend infinity. God is, as is the life He sustains, beyond probability. An anecdote about Albert Einstein demonstrates why complexity, including a complex God, cannot always be simplified.

One day a pesky reporter asked Einstein to describe his theory of relativity in a few simple words. He responded with

---

11. God cannot even be accurately reduced to one gender, as God carries both male and female attributes. (For example, "So God created man in his own image, in the image of God he created him; male and female he created them" *Genesis*, chapter 1.) Unfortunately, the non-gender alternative pronoun in English is It, an impersonal state that mucks up the picture even more than He. Where plausible, to avoid cumbersome phrasing, I'll use He. Substitute She if you prefer. In the interest of stability, I won't be cross-naming.

the following story. A man was asked by a blind man to describe the color white. The man said, "White is the color of a swan." The blind man said, "What is a swan?" The man said, "A swan is a bird with a crooked neck."

The blind man asked, "What is crooked?" The man was becoming impatient. He grabbed the blind man's arm, straightened it and said, "This is straight." Then he bent it and said, "And this is crooked."

Whereupon the blind man quickly said, "Yes, yes, thank you. Now I know what white is."

Our questions about God, and to God, can take on a similar surreal quality. Are there any questions God cannot answer? All nonsense questions are unanswerable. Is it farther to New York or by bus? Is purple square or round? What's the difference between a toad? How can I live forever without plugging into the source of life? C. S. Lewis points out that most of our metaphysical questions are like these.

We spend too much effort braying our infallibility rather than bridling our strutting tongues. When I was starting to seriously seek God, my friend Larry Smith undertook to "study with me." He and I met in his house to look into the Bible and to talk about my doubts, and I asked Larry some hard questions: "What happens to aborted babies? How does God 'answer' our prayers for others and still honor their freedom of choice? Why does God allow so much suffering?"

To each question Larry provided a stunning answer. "I don't know," he said.

I couldn't believe it. I thought Christians presumed they knew everything. This was the one answer he could have given that appealed to me. Then he added, "I have some ideas, but whenever I don't reach satisfying conclusions, I pick that question up and hang it on a hook at the back of my mind. Later, I'll take it down and look at it again." He smiled his wry, tilted smile. "No matter how much I think I know, I want to keep growing."

God is a humbling mystery, but a mystery isn't something we know nothing about; it's something we don't know everything about.[12] We choose the smooth downhill path when we choose gods who will not trouble us with the fact of evil or the problem of suffering, when life's perplexing contradictions are evaded and dismissed. Designer gods persuade us to pick daffodils, live and let live, and to speak of love as though it were an easy thing, subject to no more disciplined effort than a stroll in a meadow. Unfortunately, though, the world is a tough place. Marriages burst at the seams. People die from mistaken impressions. Dark flames of rage and despair lick about us. Living for God or the god-of-my-perceptions is the difference between fighting an insanely hot inferno with a fire hose or a can of diet cola.

As you read through this book, take what makes sense, cover it within your coat, and toss the rest away, or simply hang the remainder on a hook at the back of your mind to be explored later. Too many people have surrendered their search for truth because they became riddled by a tumor of doubt.

Our great need is to recognize our great need. And our deepest need burrows to the core of our lives.

Saying the "s" word

Humankind's deepest need is one we fight against most feverishly. From birth till death, we dodge and disavow it. I don't like it at all. Though virtually everyone talks a good game of love

---

12. We don't fully know *ourselves.* After Jesus disclosed that one of His closest friends would betray Him, the disciples asked, "Is it I?" They weren't certain of their own hidden motives.

and justice, we are essentially selfish creatures. We are born self-ish, nurtured in selfishness, seduced by selfishness, rewarded for selfishness—and prone to deny it. The ancient Greeks called it *hubris,* a fatal flaw of pride. The Bible calls it sin.

We don't perceive our true condition because our self-centered atmosphere flows through our veins. Does a fish *feel* wet? We are immersed in self-absorption. Addicted to our-selves, we can't kick the habit. An alien virus has impregnated the planet, warping our perceptions until goodness appears strange and evil tastes good. Jesus says, "The eye is the lamp of the body. So, if your eye is sound, your whole body will be full of light; but if your eye is not sound, your whole body will be full of darkness. If then the light in you is darkness, how great is the darkness!"

Becky Pippert details her pilgrimage away from insisting on her own innocence:

> Slowly I started acknowledging my own faults. I began to deal with the root problems in my life and not merely the symptoms. I saw that my pride and self-centeredness lay deep within, far deeper than I had ever imagined. And I made an exciting discov-ery. The more I faced myself—my self-deceptions, pockets of unbelief, false confidences, controlling de-vices, and so on—the more I found freedom.

Once my wife Yolanda and I were waiting on a plane pre-paring to fly from Baltimore to Dallas. The flight was delayed after boarding, so we sat on the plane for an hour and a half. During the wait a man in front of us fell into a sound sleep. With the announcement that, owing to mechanical difficulties, the plane would not be departing, scores of disgruntled passengers grabbed their overhead bags and began exiting the aircraft. Startled, the man awoke with an expression so comical it activated Yolanda's shaking, silent laugh for about five minutes. The poor red-eyed fellow looked around, perplexed, and peered out the window, but he couldn't straightway tell where he was because all terminals look the same. *Was he in Dallas, or was he still in Baltimore?*[13]

Many of us look at "salvation" that way: Have we arrived, or are we still waiting for the trip? Is my life all right as it is? Can I tell by the people around me if I'm sitting on the right flight? One problem in our culture is we don't know we're lost. The other problem is we don't know we're found.

Our situation is something like walking out the back door of a house and plunging painfully down a deep pit someone dug during the night. We can't climb out; it's too slick and too steep. No one can hear our calls for help. There we sit, nursing our wounds and cursing our fortune. Suddenly a rope drops down from above. "Hold on!" a voice cries. "I'll pull you out."

Now, we may respond in many ways. We can say, "I didn't ask to be down here. It's not my fault I'm in this dank, smelly pit. So forget the rope. I'm not taking it."

We can say, "If you know where I am, you must have had something to do with digging this pit, so I'm not trusting you. No way."

We can say, "I'll accept the rope only if *I* can pull myself out. I don't want any help from you." But pulling ourselves up proves futile. It's much too far. After a few tries, we drop to the bottom. "Thanks for nothing!" we wheeze.

---

13. He eventually figured it out.

Or we can hold on. It takes effort to keep our hold, but when at last we reach the surface, eyes stinging from fresh light, lungs filling with fresh air, we drop to our knees. "Thank you!" we gasp. "I was afraid no one would ever hear me or help me. I was afraid I'd be stuck there."

"You're welcome, my child," God says, wrapping us up in His arms.

Imagine what it would be like in such a situation for a parent to ask a child to hold on, and for the child to refuse, eventually perishing. What agony for that parent! No amount of begging or enticing can bring the child to a welcoming warm embrace. God endures this scene with His children every hour.

Some people believe that God is selective, choosing only those who cozy up to Him to curry His favor. In reality, salvation has nothing to do with favoritism and everything to do with substance. In our present condition we can't bear God's presence just as we can't stare at the sun without going blind. Sin is separation from God, rebellion against God, and the results are sins. Preaching that sin is "offensive" to God stops short of disclosing the true problem: not that sin offends God so much as sin hurts living beings, including God. Sin and suffering are "sinonyms." When we separate ourselves from God we *inevitably* cause pain; it's as predictable as the moon's phases. That's the sin problem—all the hurt in history can be chalked up to it. Who in their right minds wouldn't be against that? However, what we are reluctant to accept is the tendency toward decrying some sins and overlooking others, picketing abortion clinics while keeping silent about tens of millions killed by promoting tobacco use overseas. Or claiming that matters of taste are sinful. As horrible as sin is, it's gotten a bad rap whenever it's been twisted into something else.

We are especially uncomfortable with guilt. Listen to people discuss guilt in general and one message comes through with conviction: guilt is bad But it's those who feel *no* guilt who are most dangerous—the psychopathic liars and killers, Nuremberg war criminals, and hatemongers of the world who feel totally justified in their ghastly acts. In August, 1969, a small cult under the hypnotic direction of Charles Manson brutally slaughtered seven people in what became known as the Tate-LaBianca murders. At his trial, after the court found him guilty, Manson was asked if he had any comments before the judge handed down his sentence. Wild-eyed and scraggly, Manson stood, pointed to the jury and seethed, "You have no right to try me! I did what I felt was right!"

Don't we all insist this for ourselves? No matter what heinous lie or hatred we have perpetrated, we long to absolve ourselves of blame, twirling and ducking to avoid the penetrating missile of guilt. But guilt in itself is not bad. It's faulty guilt that's tragic. It's unresolved guilt that's deadly. Without guilt—that discomforting twinge of conscience—we would be a sorrier race than we are now. As long as we're convinced we have never done anything wrong, we can never do anything right. We complain to God that we're uncomfortable, and God turns to us with a sad smile and says, "Good." How else would we change our lack of compassion, our critical spirit, our greed, our desire for revenge? Paradoxically, while each of us is—*just as we are*—a priceless gift of infinite worth, none of us is "OK." We're all struggling people who need help.

What of the undeniable good that flares in us? Hear the magnificent strings of a live orchestra or the spine-tingling cheers from the crowd at Special Olympics. Acts of unselfish sacrifice and heroism can be witnessed every day, from exhausted mothers working overtime to firefighters dying to save the life of a ninety-year-old. Insisting on our own innocence, though, is futile. As C. S. Lewis points out, "Everyone feels benevolent if nothing happens to be annoying him at the moment." Joseph Cooke remarks, "I have never heard of any large group of people who, without external pressure or necessity, willingly agreed together to suffer major inconvenience or loss for the benefit of other groups who were worse off. . . . When the chips are down expediency always wins out over morality." Throughout history the "good" people, saints and prophets, reformers and martyrs, have found that the closer they get to truth and to God, the clearer they see cruelty, selfishness, and deception crouching in us all. Literature mirrors this finding. The same conclusion is reached in *Hamlet, A Separate Peace, The Fall, Crime and Punishment,* and hundreds of other stories.

In William Golding's *Lord of the Flies,* an idyllic uninhabited island absorbs a crashed planeload of British schoolboys. With no adults on hand, Ralph and Piggy attempt to construct a "civilized" structure, but when Jack and his minions counter, the result is horrifying death. Their new society is peopled from eggs of the serpent's brood. Perhaps as much as any book, *Lord of the Flies* (an alias for Beelzebub, or Satan) plays out the futile quest for lasting peace and love if it is based only upon human instincts. Rousseau's "noble savage" ideal is torched with the boys' island.

Our situation is like a doctor informing us, "You must stop smoking. Plain and simple, it's killing you. You need to slow down—your blood pressure is too high. If you don't start eating less and exercising more, you're a prime candidate for a heart attack."

Some people respond, "I gotta find me another doctor."

What about you? Your conscience can be saying, "My life is out of control—it's running away from me. I feel empty and tired too often. My relationships are superficial, my promises are ropes of sand, my existence lacks purpose. The joy is seeping from my life."

It happens to all of us. We may have done something so bad we didn't think it was possible for us to do it. The realization hits, *I need something more. Or maybe Someone more.*

What then?

Self-deception is at the base of sin's affliction. Our need is not first to avoid sin but to recognize sin. Gary Krause comments, "The last thing we need is another New Age book, cassette, lecture, or video on discovering the god within and unleashing our innate goodness. The last thing we need is another slick millionaire self-help guru telling us how wonderful we are." Attempting to fix the sin problem ourselves when we *are* the problem is like our hearing from the bank that our checking account is overdrawn, and responding, "That's all right. Here, I'll write a check to cover it."

Often sinning is a natural reflex, like sticking your tongue into the hole left by a recently departed tooth. "Sinning is not very creative," notes Charles Sandefur, "it's generally the same dish served over and over." One definition of sin is the refusal to grow, the stubborn determination to go our own way. We really want to be God. Though it's fashionable to shrug off extramarital affairs and depict desserts as "decadently sinful," winning the war against sin involves more than swearing off chocolate cheesecake.

A pretty good person

Basically I think I'm a pretty good person. Unfortunately,

I can also think that the glacier makes a peachy spot for a picnic. What matters is how God views us. The Bible says that God "sees not as man sees; man looks on the outward appearance, but the Lord looks on the heart."

In the film *Places in the Heart* a gang of hooded Klansmen are beating Moze, a black sharecropper, senseless until his friend, blind Mr. Will, starts calling out their names. "That's Mr. Thompson, I been selling him brooms for years. Sure as you're Mr. Shaw. And that's Mr. Simmons over there by the barn." The Klansmen know the game is up. Their hooded masks don't fool Mr. Will, because he knows them by another sense.

Our pretty good masks don't hoodwink God. God knows the germ within. He recognizes us not only by our actions, but by the DNA of our thoughts. God views us through His electron microscope and rubs His brow in sorrow. "This virus is a million times deadlier than AIDS," He sighs. "No living being can survive it. If it's unleashed in the universe, it will be hell."

G. K. Chesterton understood this. Many years ago *The Times* of London headlined the question, "What's Wrong with the World?" Chesterton responded in the letters section with characteristic directness: "I am. Yours truly, G. K. Chesterton."

How hard can it be to live and love perfectly? People who don't know music can't appreciate the subtleties or the difficulties inherent in a Mozart movement. The same is true with playing out godly purity, patience, faithfulness, self-control. I remember reading for the first time the following words from C. S. Lewis in *Mere Christianity* and being startled into a new comprehension of my condition:

> No man knows how bad he is till he has tried
> very hard to be good. A silly idea is current that

good people do not know what temptation means. This is an obvious lie. Only those who try to resist temptation know how strong it is. After all, you find out the strength. . . of a wind by trying to walk against it, not by lying down. A man who gives in to temptation after five minutes simply does not know what it would have been like an hour later.

That is why bad people, in one sense, know very little about badness. They have lived a sheltered life by always giving in. We never find out the strength of the evil impulse inside us until we try to fight it: and Christ, because He was the only man who never yielded to temptation, is also the only man who knows to the full what temptation means—the only complete realist.

We are like skydivers plummeting from a great height with parachutes strapped to our backs. No matter how comfortable we become during the fall, shouting to each other over the turbulence, doing loop-de-loops, enjoying the wind in our hair, our end is certain death. The one way to survive is to admit we need a parachute. And when we pull the ripcord, we suddenly leave the crowd.

For those who are honestly searching and who earnestly desire what is right, who have sensed something we cannot shake from our minds, during those times when we feel totally empty a living being enters the void to fill what only He can fill. Dag Hammarskjold concludes, "When you have nothing left but God you will become aware for the first time that God is enough."

▲ ▼ ▲

Jerry Levin served as a news correspondent in the Middle East boiling pot of Beirut when in an instant his life changed drastically. Walking to work one March morning in 1984, he felt a tap on his shoulder. Turning, he faced a young bearded man who pushed a handgun into Levin's stomach, propelling him toward a gray car with an open rear door. Levin didn't resist. He slid into the seat as the assailant jumped in beside him.

"Close eyes! Close eyes!" the man shouted. "You see, I kill." The car sped away. For the next eleven months, Levin, a fifty-one-year-old grandfather, was held hostage, blindfolded and chained to a wall in a tiny room. He was a Jewish agnostic, caught in the crossfire of fanatic religious terrorism. While in his prison, with no literature, no preachers, no tender counsel, no human interference of any kind, Levin became a believer in God. In fact, he became a Christian.

Outside, his wife had been praying fervently for him. Muslim, Jewish, and Christian friends joined in working for his release. One Muslim leader in Beirut commented that never in the past thousand years had so many people of differing faiths worked together on behalf of one man. On February 13, 1985, Levin wrestled out of his chain, lowered himself from his window, and escaped his captors.

"The irony," Levin said later, "is that all those people thought they were working for someone who was a godless man. . . I am convinced now that none of us is ever really godless. I know now that God is there for us whether or not we are there for God."

The wild truth is that God is there for us.